4 50

WARSHIP MONOGRAPHS
QUEEN ELIZABETH CLASS

H.M.S. Warspite October 1920

WARSHIP MONOGRAPHS

QUEEN ELIZABETH CLASS

John Campbell

CONWAY MARITIME PRESS
1972

© Conway Maritime Press Ltd. 1972
7 Nelson Road, Greenwich, London. S.E.10

ISBN 085177 052 5

Printed in Great Britain by
Latimer Trend & Co. Ltd
Whitstable Kent

Contents

The publishers wish to acknowledge with thanks the following:—
The National Maritime Museum for the photographs on pages 31 and 37 and Commander Joel for the photographs on pages 20, 21, 22 and 30.

All line drawings in this series by John A. Roberts. By courtesy of A and A Plans, London.

Illustrations and Plans

Introduction

The ships of the *Queen Elizabeth* class were perhaps the most famous of all British steam propelled battleships, and as originally completed with two well-proportioned funnels they were among the most handsome. They gave excellent service in the First World War, and after large alterations which in three of the five amounted almost to rebuilding, did the same in 1939–1945.

In this monograph the ships are considered in their First World War state as they were then in the forefront of warship design, whereas if the Washington Treaty of 1922 had not put a stop to the normal process of capital ship development, they would have been obsolete long before 1939, no matter how much they had been reconstructed.

Queen Elizabeth, Portsmouth 1915

SHIPS OF THE CLASS

The five ships of the class, which were the last battleships designed under Sir Philip Watts as Director of Naval Construction, were built as set out in the table of general particulars opposite.

The first four were built under the 1912-13 Estimates, while the *Malaya* was a gift of the Federated Malay States. A sixth ship of the type to be built at Portsmouth under the 1914—15 Estimates was cancelled. The main details of the design to which they were built were:

	LAID DOWN	LAUNCHED	COMPLETED	BUILT
QUEEN ELIZABETH	21 Oct 1912	16 Oct 1913	Jan 1915	Portsmouth
WARSPITE	31 Oct 1912	26 Nov 1913	Mar 1915	Devonport
BARHAM	24 Feb 1913	31 Dec 1914	Oct 1915	John Brown
VALIANT	31 Jan 1913	4 Nov 1914	Feb 1916	Fairfield
MALAYA	20 Oct 1913	18 Mar 1915	Feb 1916	Armstrong

Dimensions: 600-ft (p.p.), 634½-ft (w.l.) x 90-ft 6-ins x 28-ft 9-ins (mean at normal load). Sinkage 98 tons per inch.
Displacement: 27,500 tons normal, 31,534 tons deep load.
Main Armament: 8 x 15-in 42 calibre in 4 twin turrets, superfiring pairs fore and aft.
Secondary Armament: 16 x 6-in Mark XII — 12 in an upper deck battery forward, 4 in a main deck battery aft. Also 2 x 3-in AA, 4 x 21-in submerged TT.
Armour Belt: 13—6-in between end barbettes, 6—4-in forward and aft, 6—4-in bulkheads.
Turrets: 13—11-in with 5-in or 4½-in crowns.
Barbettes: 10—7-in above decks, reduced to 6—4-in at middle deck.
Battery: 6-in.
Conning Tower: 11-in with 3-in crown.

Decks: Forecastle: 1-in over battery. Upper: 2—1¼-in between end barbettes. Main: 1¼-in over belt ends. Middle: 1-in between end barbettes, 2½-in, 1¼-in for short distances aft. Lower: 3—1-in forward, 3—2½-in aft.
Torpedo Bulkhead: 2-in.
Boilers: 24 large tube, Yarrow type in *Warspite* and *Barham;* Babcock and Wilcox in others.
Engines: 4 shaft turbines, Brown Curtis in *Barham* and *Valiant.* Parsons in others.
SHP and Speed: Normal full power 56,000 = 23 kts; designed overload 72,000 = 25 kts. Astern 30,000.
Fuel: Oil only. 650 tons at normal displacement, 3,400 tons at deep load.
Metacentric Height: (With free surface correction) 5.7-in at normal displacement, 6.9-ft at deep load.
Estimated weights at normal displacement: Hull 8.900 tons. Armament (including turret shields) 4,550. Armour and protective plating 8.600. Machinery (incl. engineer's stores, not reserve feed water) 3,950. General equipment 750, oil fuel 650. Margin 100.

DESIGN

The outstanding novelties of the design were the introduction of the 15-inch gun, the use of oil fuel only in a capital ship, and as far as the British Navy was concerned, the combination of battleship protection with a speed of 25 kts, though the German battlecruisers *Seydlitz* and *Derfflinger* had priority here and were also faster.

In criticising the above design the first fact to be noted is that the displacement was too small, and all were well over the designed figure as completed, when their actual deep load displacements were:

Queen Elizabeth, 33,020; *Warspite,* 33,410; *Barham,* 32,910; *Valiant,* 33,280; *Malaya,* 33,220;

in good agreement with the figure in official lists of 29,150 tons for the normal displacement of the class. By September 1917 the deep load displacements had increased to:

Queen Elizabeth, 34,050; *Warspite,* 33,670; ▷

3

▷ *Barham*, 33,590; *Valiant*, 33,910; *Malaya*, 33,530;

and it was usual to limit the oil fuel to about 2,800 tons. The original excess weights were incurred from a number of alterations, among which were the stiffening of the fore part of the hull by extra girders etc. behind the side plating, the provision of additional girders under the forecastle deck in way of blast from the forward 15-inch guns, 2-in centre-line bulkheads in the 6-in batteries, a large number of valves in the ventilation system to protect the water-tight compartmentation, and arrangements to correct listing of the ship by pumping oil to the higher side, and by flooding certain water-tight compartments. The frames in the forward part of the hull were more widely spaced in this class than in most of their predecessors, and the *Colossus* had broken two frames right forward in a heavy sea, while a brief experience of the effect of under-water weapons had shown the need for the additional valves and flooding arrangements mentioned above. By September 1917 as a result of the Battle of Jutland, additional safety devices were installed for the 15-in and 6-in ammunition, the middle deck over the magazines and the glacis plates of the forward 6-in battery were thickened by 1-inch, as were the athwartships bulkheads adjacent to the end 15-in magazines. Director firing for the 6-in guns was also fitted, and by the end of the war flying platforms for aircraft were installed on the superfiring turrets.

The reasons for the different increases in displacement between completion and September 1917 are not fully known, but the *Queen Elizabeth* had been hurried into service and had not been finished to the usual standards. The effect of excess weight was chiefly felt in the immersion of the 13-in belt and in the loss of speed, as the heights above water of the heavy guns — 'A' turret 30-ft 9-ins, 'B' 40-ft 9-ins, 'X' 33-ft 3-ins, 'Y' 23-ft 3-ins at designed normal displacement — were greater than in German ships and an additional draught of 2-ft or so for a given fuel loading not very serious, though it may be noted that at 34,000 tons the upper deck was only 11-ft above water amidships.

An equivalent German design of April 1916 would have had a normal displacement of c. 33,500 tons and in spite of a beam of 98.4-ft, a water-line length to beam ratio of 7.33 as against 7.01 in the *Queen Elizabeths*, and there seems no doubt that the latter were too short for 25 kt ships. With regard to the limitation of beam in British designs, ships of over 100-ft beam could be accommodated in the dockyard at Rosyth from the early summer of 1915, and in 1914 such a ship could have been docked at Portsmouth, and also in two floating docks if under 32,000 tons, though 90-ft 6-ins was about the limit for the dry docks at Devonport, Gibraltar and Malta. A truer reason for the *Queen Elizabeths'* beam of ▷

H.M.S. Malaya 1917

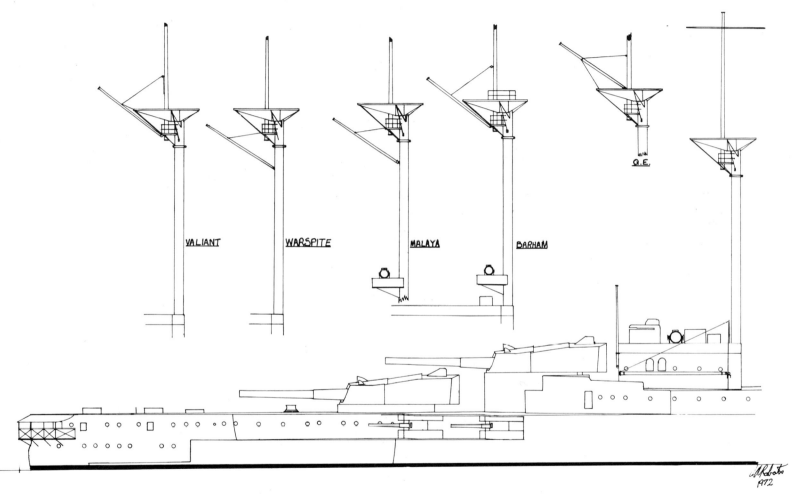

VALIANT   WARSPITE   MALAYA   BARHAM

Q.E.

Queen Elizabeth as completed. Sternwalk removed 1916. 6″ guns aft removed 1915 or 1916. Gaff fitted (as inset) 1916 or 17. Barham was fitted with a sternwalk in 1919. Other vessels similar except as insets. Gaffs fitted in others 1916. Sternwalk and 6″ guns aft not fitted in others.

Queen Elizabeth as completed. Others similar except as inset. Left: Only Queen Elizabeth and Barham were completed with 2nd yard on fore topmast — this being removed from both in 1916. Queen Elizabeth and Barham were fitted with a flagstaff on the fore topmast in 1916 (see main drawing of Queen Elizabeth.) The platform under the fore top in the main drawing of Queen Elizabeth was fitted in 1916/17. Below: Barham as completed. All were completed with search light towers on after funnel as shown. In 1917 these towers were increased in height and two more were added, one each side of the funnel, as shown in the main drawing of Queen Elizabeth. In the case of Valiant and Warspite (and possibly the others) the new towers were added some time after the originals were raised. All were completed with a 6″ gun on each side amidships, as shown, except Queen Elizabeth which had hers fitted in 1915 or 1916. The 6″ guns amidships were removed from all five in 1916.

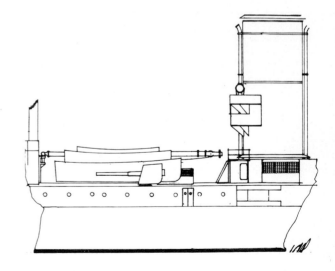

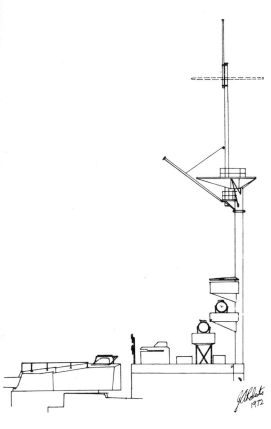

Barham 1919. All fitted with main topmast 1919 (except Queen Elizabeth which was already so fitted.) Barham and Queen Elizabeth with flagstaff on topmast 1919.

▷ 90-ft 6-ins was the wish to avoid too great a metacentric height which it was feared might lead to an unsteady gun platform, and in the next British battleships of the *Royal Sovereign* class, the beam was actually reduced to 88-ft 6-ins.

ARMAMENT

The main armament of eight 15-inch in four twin turrets was ideal at the time, and better than nine such guns in triples. The German *Bayern* in service more than a year after the *Queen Elizabeth*, also had eight 15-inch and there is no doubt that this was preferable to the twelve 14-inch in four triples of the American *Pennsylvania*, the 12 14-inch in six twins of the Japanese twelve 14-inch in six twins of the Japanese *Fuso* and the twelve or sixteen 13.4-inch in quadruple turrets of French designs. The 15-inch gun was of the usual British wire-wound type with Welin stepped screw breech, and made exceptionally good shooting. Details of it and of contemporary foreign guns were:

The greater weight of the British gun compared to the German was not entirely a disadvantage as it reduced the recoil energy, and the heavier shell and lower muzzle velocity were the better choice, the two guns having comparable muzzle energies.

The British 15-in twin mounting was also very good, and more compact than the German with an internal barbette diameter of 30-ft 6-ins as against 32-ft 10-ins. The total revolving weight was about 770 tons. Training and elevation, hoists, loading rammers and breeches were worked hydraulically, the necessary power being provided by 4 steam driven pumps and piped to the turrets. As was the rule in British battleships of the time, the shell rooms were on the hold deck and the magazines on the platform deck, though tests later showed that the opposite disposition was to be preferred. The lower hoists led to the working chamber where shells and charges were transferred to the gun loading cages of the upper hoists. The chain loading rammers were fitted on the end of the gun slides, and loading could take place up to ▷

Gun	Length of Bore	Weight of Gun	Weight of Shell	Muzzle Velocity
British 15-in	42 calibres	100 tons	1.920 lbs	2,475 f.s.
German 15-in	42.4 calibres	76.3 tons	1.653 lbs	2.625 f.s.
U.S.A. 14-in	45 calibres	63.5 tons	1,400 lbs	2,600 f.s.
Japanese 14-in	45 calibres	83.5 tons	1,485 lbs	2,525 f.s.

▷ the maximum elevation of 20°. The range at this elevation with 1914–1918 projectiles was 24,300 yards, which was fully adequate for North Sea conditions and greater than that of any contemporary German ship as originally completed. The maximum rate of fire, which was not likely to be employed in battle, was as high as 2 rounds per gun per minute, and 100 rounds per gun were carried. Four-gun salvos (one gun in each turret) were the rule, and not full salvos. There were two directors, one protected by 6-in armour on the conning tower roof and the other in the fore top, and five 15-ft range-finders, one in each turret and one in the armoured director tower.

There were certain defects in the 15-in turrets, which were remedied during the course of the First World War. By far the most serious was that the precautions against the flash of a charge ignited somewhere in the turret structure reaching the magazines, were not adequate to deal with the violent behaviour of the British cordite charges, which were in single silk bags with a 16-oz. fine grain black powder igniter for each quarter charge. This danger, to which all British battleships and battlecruisers were liable, was not fully appreciated until three battlecruisers blew up from this cause at the Battle of Jutland, and adequate safety measures were introduced as soon as possible after the battle.

The lack of stop and non-return valves in the hydraulic exhaust system was another defect revealed at Jutland that applied to other ships as well, and when the Queen Elizabeth entered service her guns were not sighted beyond 15°, and the necessary range data not available from 15° to 20° This was however remedied by 1916.

A further unfortunate matter which concerned all British heavy guns was the poor quality of the armour-piercing shells which suffered from having too hard and brittle heads and too sensitive a burster, Lyddite (picric acid) being used. It was known perfectly well before the war that these shells were unlikely to pierce heavy armour and burst inside, but nothing was done until after Jutland, and although a vastly improved armour piercing shell was developed, it was not until 12 December 1918 that the 15-in gun battleships had even 30% of their outfit in this type of shell.

With regard to the secondary armament the four guns in the after main deck battery were very soon found to be useless and were only mounted in the Queen Elizabeth as originally completed. They were replaced in all of the class by two guns in open-backed shields on the forecastle deck forward of the main mast. The 6-in Mark XII was a satisfactory gun firing a 100-lb shell with a muzzle velocity of 2,825 f.s. and a range of 13,500 yards at 14° elevation. They were in hand worked pedestal mountings and could fire at 7 rounds or more per minute, but the ammunition supply was far from equalling this rate. The principal 6-in magazines and shell rooms were between those of 'B' turret and the foremost boiler room, and two dredgers and two other hoists supplied the twelve battery guns which were separated by 1½-in screens running about 15-ft inboard and divided into port and starboard batteries by a 2-in centre-line bulkhead. As the above hoists could only supply about 3 rounds per gun, a considerable amount of ready ammunition was needed, and as described below, this nearly caused the loss of the Malaya at Jutland. Safety measures were introduced after this battle, and two more dredger hoists subsequently fitted. The 6-in ammunition allowance was 150 round per gun, reduced to 116 after Jutland to compensate for some of the weight added. A temporary 6-in director was installed in the Queen Elizabeth in late 1916, and the complete 6-in director in March 1917 in this ship, and in April-July 1917 for the rest of the class. The original centreline direction was replaced in 1917 by two, port and starboard on the forward superstructure. In German capital ships the 5.9-in guns of the secondary armament had side and rear screens forming individual casemates, each of which was supplied by a dredger hoist from a magazine, that contained shells and charges, and fed one or at most two guns. This seems a better system, though it was difficult to find space for the numerous small magazines required.

Anti-aircraft defence was of little import- ▷

ance to ships in 1914—1918 and the two 3-in guns provided were quite adequate. A.A. guns were in very short supply in 1915 and the *Queen Elizabeth* originally had one 3-in and one 3-pdr. Whether the provision of four 21-in submerged torpedo tubes, two of which were just forward of 'A' magazines and two just aft of 'Y', can be justified, must be a matter of opinion. As many as 20 torpedoes could be carried, but the pattern available in early 1915 only had a 280-lb wet gun-cotton charge, and though 400-lb Amatol charges were later provided, it does not appear that torpedoes with 500-lb charges issued to battlecruisers, light cruisers and destroyers were supplied to any battleships in the First World War. The torpedoes carried by the *Queen Elizabeth* class had a range of 10,000—10,750 yards at 28 kts or in the case of some, 15,000 at 24 and 18,500 at 19 kts. Only two, one by the *Valiant* and one by the *Malaya* were fired at an enemy ship.

PROTECTION

The armour protection was not really adequate for a 15-in gunned battleship that must be expected sooner or later to engage ships with guns of similar power. Far too much reliance was placed on 6-in armour which was too thin against even German 11-in guns. At the designed normal draught of 28-ft 9-ins the main belt extended from 9-ft above water to 4-ft below, but the maximum thickness of 13-ins which ▷

15" Gun Breech

was reduced to 8-ins at the lower edge, only extended to 4-ft 6-ins above water and was then tapered to 6-ins at main deck level. Thus at an actual fighting draught of 32-ft 9-ins only 6-ins of the 13-ins armour were above water and the 6-in upper edge of the main belt was as low as 5-ft above water. The *Royal Sovereigns* which followed the *Queen Elizabeths* and were generally considered inferior, at least had 12-ft 9-ins of 13-in armour, though a designed displacement that was unrealistically low in this class as well removed much of its value.

Above the main belt the *Queen Elizabeths* had 6-in armour to the upper deck. The value of this was doubtful, and though the British 12-in gun dreadnoughts had no side armour above the main deck, the 13.5-in ships with 12-in maximum belts, had 8-in. The later German battleships with 14-in maximum belts had 8-in or 10-in upper belts, and the corresponding battle-cruisers 12-in maximum belts tapering to 9-in at the upper deck. On the other hand American battleships laid down from 1912, had 13½-in maximum belts and no side armour above the main deck, but this deck was 3-in or 3½-in thick, and it may be said in conclusion the *Queen Elizabeths* do not compare well with their contemporaries in the matter of amidships side protection.

It so happened that no really damaging shell hits forward of 'A' barbette were made in any British ship at Jutland, while the Germans suffered badly from hits in this position, the *Lutzow's* sinking being attributable to this cause. The German solution in their projected designs of much larger displacement, was to take the heavy belt well past the end barbettes and improve the subdivision forward by removing the broadside torpedo tubes. The first was impossible in a ship of the *Queen Elizabeth's* size, and the 6 – 4-in armour forward and aft was probably justifiable, as were the bulk-heads of this thickness.

The turret armour was satisfactory with a 13-in face plate and 11-in sides and rear, while the crowns were 5-in in the first four ships of the class, and 4¼-in of a tougher quality steel in the *Malaya*. For comparison the *Bayern's* turrets had 14-in faces, 10-in sides and 11½-in rears with a 4-in flat crown and 8 – 4¾-in sloping plates joining this to the vertical armour. The *Pennsylvania's* turrets had 18-in faces, 10 – 9-in sides, 9-in rears and 5-in crowns, and this was perhaps a more logical distribution of thickness, though the side and rear of turrets were hit at Jutland in German ships. The barbettes in the *Queen Elizabeths* were seriously under-protected, though they were no worse than in other British dreadnoughts. An armour thickness of 12-in or 13-in instead of 10-in should have been provided and a reduction to only 7-in where the barbettes partly shielded each other, was also unsatisfactory. In the *Bayern* the barbettes were 14 – 19-in above decks, and were reduced much as in British ships where behind side or battery armour, while in the *Pennsylvania* they were 13-in or 13½-in to the main deck and 4½-in to the middle deck.

The protection given to the 6-in guns, and the conning tower does not call for comment, and the deck thicknesses were much as in German ships, though very thin by post 1918 standards, and in fact also by the requirements of 1914. All previous British dreadnoughts had longitudinal screen bulkheads protecting the ammunition spaces and in some the middle but not the wing, engine rooms, while in others these bulkheads were continuous between end barbettes, but so far inboard forward and aft that they only protected the ammunition spaces here. The *Queen Elizabeths* were the first British ships with a torpedo bulkhead that protected the whole of the ship between end barbettes. The detailed construction was determined as a result of two experiments on the old turret ship *Hood* which had been completed in 1893, and had a length of 2-ft longitudinal bulkhead built into her for the trials. As a result it was decided to have the 2-in bulkhead 10-ft from the *Queen Elizabeth's* side with a thin longitudinal bulkhead inboard of this, except by the wing engine rooms which were directly inboard of the 2-in bulkhead. According to German practice which was based on a long series of trials, this construction was wrong and it was better to have the thick torpedo bulkhead in the inner ▷

position with the thin bulkhead outboard of it. The Germans also found that the skin plating should be reduced in thickness to lessen the 'projectile effect' of large fragments blown in by the torpedo explosion.

A serious criticism was the lack of pumping capacity unless the main circulating pumps were used on bilge position. In each boiler room there was only one fire and bilge pump and one ejector with a combined capacity of 275 tons an hour, while in the *Benbow* and *Emperor of India* the figure per boiler room was 1,100 tons in 1916 due principally to two ash-expeller pumps. Large 'salvage' pumps which were fitted in German ships — there were 6 of 900 tons per hour each, in the *Bayerns* – were absent and the total capacity of such pumps in the *Queen Elizabeth* was only 950 tons per hour.

The metacentric height was greater than usual in British capital ships of the period, and considerably larger than in the *Royal Sovereigns* and the *Hood*. This was a good feature, and it was probably quite sufficient, though in German ships 8½ ft was general, and in the *Seydlitz* it was a little over 10-ft. □

H.M.S. Warspite October 1920

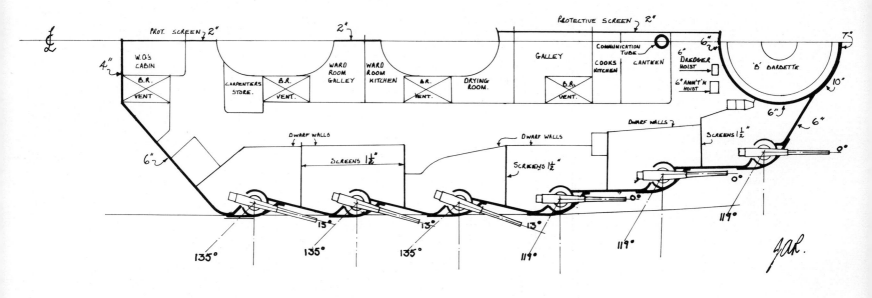

PROT. SCREEN 2"
W.O's CABIN
B.R.
VENT
4"
6"
CARPENTERS STORE.
B.R.
VENT.
2"
WARD ROOM GALLEY
WARD ROOM KITCHEN
B.R.
VENT.
DRYING ROOM.
GALLEY
PROTECTIVE SCREEN 2"
COMMUNICATION TUBE
COOKS KITCHEN
CANTEEN
B.R.
VENT.
6" DREDGER HOIST
6" AMM'T'N HOIST
6" 2"
'B' BARBETTE
7"
10"
6"
6"
DWARF WALLS
SCREENS 1½"
DWARF WALLS
SCREENS 1½"
DWARF WALLS
SCREENS 1½"
SCREENS 1½"
0°
0°
0°
15°
13°
13°
119°
119°
119°
135°
135°
135°
119°
JAR.

G.A OF St.b. 6" BATTERY.   R.U. 6" SHELLS WERE STOWED
AGAINST THE SIDE SCREENS AND DWARF WALLS (23 TO 38 shells/Casemate)

MACHINERY

The criticisms would mostly have entailed additional weight, but the machinery was rather heavy by German standards. The 24 large-tube boilers were in four rooms and supplied steam at 235-lb per square inch. There were three engine rooms with two sets of turbines. In the ships with Parsons turbines the high pressure ahead and high pressure astern turbines were on the wing shafts, and the low pressure ahead and astern in one casing on the inner shafts, and there were also geared cruising turbines at the forward end of each high pressure turbine which were clutched out at high speed. Otherwise all the turbines in the class were direct drive. In the two ships with Brown-Curtis turbines, the high pressure ahead and the low pressure ahead and astern (in one casing) were on the inner shafts, and the intermediate pressure ahead and the high pressure astern in one casing on the wing shafts. On trials the *Queen Elizabeth* was not taken above 57,130 SHP but the others developed the following:

Warspite, 77,510; *Barham*, 76,575; *Valiant*, 71,112; *Malaya*, 76,074. Accurate speeds were not taken, but when her repairs were completed after Jutland the *Barham* was tried over the mile at 32,250 tons displacement and a draught of 32-ft 6-ins forward and 33-ft aft. The average for four runs was 70,790 = 23.9 kts, and the best run 71,730 = 23.97. The *Valiant* was known to be slower at this time due to differences in her high pressure nozzles.

Figures taken for the *Queen Elizabeth* gave an oil consumption of 9.3 tons per hour at 11,000 SHP equivalent to c. 15 kts and 28 tons per hour at 55,000 SHP equivalent to c. 22 kts. The range with full oil would thus be c. 5,500 miles at 15 kts and c. 2,650 at 22, allowing no safety margin.

With regard to machinery weights it is always difficult to be sure that 'like is compared with like', but those for the *Queen Elizabeth* are given as 3,534 tons, for the *Barham* 3,582 and for the *Malaya* 4,037 as against a designed figure of 3,950 tons. The German battlecruiser *Derfflinger* developed 76,600 SHP on trials and had fourteen coal-fired and four oil-fired small tube Schulz-Thornycroft boilers with two sets of direct-drive Parsons type turbines ▷

Queen Elizabeth 1918

on 4 shafts. Full astern power was 28,000. Weights for boilers and their equipment were: *Derfflinger*, 1,342 tons; *Queen Elizabeth*, 1,534; *Barham*, 1,631; *Malaya*, 1,887.

The machinery spaces were more sub-divided in German ships, and the *Derfflinger's* boilers were in twelve compartments with four engine rooms.

In conclusion of this severe criticism of the *Queen Elizabeths* it may be said that they were a great attempt to produce a 15-in gunned 25 knot battleship on a quite inadequate displacement.

WAR SERVICE

Apart from the *Queen Elizabeth's* initial service at the Dardanelles, all five were part of the Grand Fleet from their completion to the end of the War. The *Warspite* joined in April 1915 and was at first attached to the 2nd Battle Squadron, and on 2 November after the *Queen Elizabeth* and *Barham* had joined, the 5th Battle Squadron was reconstituted for the ships of the class to act as a fast wing squadron for the battle fleet, and by March 1916 it consisted of all five ships. The *Queen Elizabeth* was in dockyard hands when Jutland was fought, but the other four took part as related below. In February 1917 the *Queen Elizabeth* ▷

A view of Valiant as completed. Note that she has an additional yard on her topmast, which was removed on entering service. She also carries an additional 6 in. gun on the forecastle deck.

H.M.S. Warspite October 1920.

1. W.T. Compartment
2. Capstan Engine Room.
3. Refrigerating and Ice making machinery compartment.
4. Meat room.
5. Canvas and cardage room.
6. Awning room.
7. Escape trunk.
8. Lobby.
9. Clothes store.
10. Cable locker.
11. Spare anchor gear.
12. Spare anchor gear
13. Carpenter's working space.
14. F.W. tank.
15. Paint store.
16. Paint room.
17. Boatswain's store.
18. Tailors workshop (port) prisons (starboard).
19. Lime store (port) sand store (starboard)
20. P.O.'s mess.
21. Sick Bay.
22. Dispensary.
23. Mess space.
24. Stores.
25. Submerged torpedo room.
26. Torpedo magazine & stores.
27. 'A' turret.
28. Ammunition trunk.
29. Storage battery compartment.
30. Space for wroking flood valves.
31. Handing room.
32. 15″ shell room.
33. 15″ magazine.
34. Telephone exchange.
35. Transmitting station.
36. 'B' Turret.
37. 6″ shell room.
38. Switchboard room.
39. 6″ magazine.
40. Lower conning tower.
41. Hydraulic machinery.
42. Conning tower.
43. Admiral's sea cabin.
44. Chart house.
45. Chart house (port) Captain's sea cabin (starboard).
46. Shelter.
47. Range finder hood.
48. Signal distributing office.
49. Bakery.
50. Navigating officer.
51. Galley.

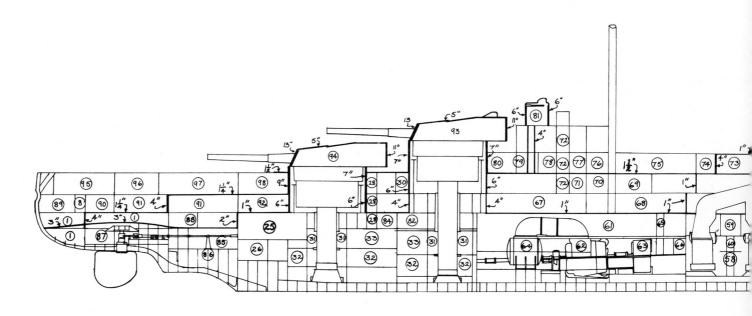

52.	Cook's kitchen.	
53.	Canteen.	
54.	Flour store.	
55.	'A' boiler room.	
56.	'B' boiler room.	
57.	'C' boiler room.	
58.	'D' boiler room.	
59.	Fan chamber.	
60.	Air lock.	
61.	Midships engine room.	
62.	L.P. Ahead and astern turbine.	
63.	H.P. Ahead turbine.	
64.	Main condenser.	
65.	Electric Lift.	
66.	Telephone cabinet.	
67.	Engineer's workshop.	
68.	Engineer's stores.	
69.	Electric boat hoist machinery	

compartment.
70. Admiral's galley.
71. W/T Office.
72. Aerial screen.
73. W.O.'s cabins.
74. Ships office and W.O.'s cabins.
75. W.O.'s mess and cabins (port) ward room (starboard).
76. Ward room Anti room (starboard) gun room (port).
77. Medical officer's cabin (starboard) gun room (port).
78. Accountant Officer's cabin (starboard) gun room (port).
79. Executive officer's cabin (starboard) engineer officer cabin (port).
80. Midshipman's study.
81. Torpedo control tower.

82. C.O.$_2$ machinery.
83. Searchlight motor generator.
84. Hydraulic machinery.
85. Steering gear compartment.
86. F.W. Tank.
87. Tiller compartment.
88. Captain's store.
89. Printing office.
90. Writer's office.
91. Cabin deck spaces.
92. Capstan motor space.
93. 'X' turret.
94. 'Y' turret.
95. Admirals day cabin.
96. Admirals dining cabin.
97. Admirals lobby.
98. Captain and Captain of Fleets cabins.

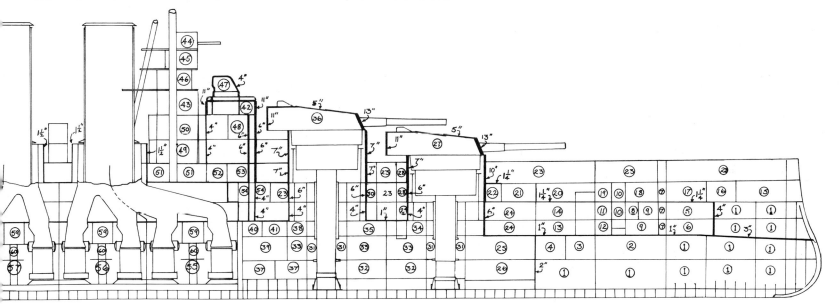

became Fleet Flagship of the Grand Fleet, while the rest continued to form the 5th BS. None of the ships were torpedoed or mined and they were only in action at the Dardanelles and at Jutland.

QUEEN ELIZABETH AT THE DARDANELLES

Far too much was expected of the *Queen Elizabeth* at the Dardanelles as it was believed that her 15-in shells would destroy the forts there as easily as the German 16.5-in howitzers had destroyed those at Antwerp. The fact that the latter's shells fell steeply on the weak overhead cover of obsolete and easily seen forts, while the *Queen Elizabeth's* would strike coastal defence works which were difficult to make out, at a relatively flat angle, was not appreciated. Also the 2,050-lb howitzer shells were designed for the attack of forts and land defences and had TNT bursters of about 240-lbs while the *Queen Elizabeth* had no such HE shells but only armour piercing with 60-lb Lyddite bursters, and common shell with 132-lbs of black powder. It might well have been better to have sent out one of the 13.5-in dreadnoughts for which HE shells were available.

It was decided that the *Queen Elizabeth* should do her gunnery trials at Gibraltar and go on to the Dardanelles. She accordingly sailed on 1 February 1915 with 3,300 tons of oil and drawing 33-ft 5-ins forward and 33-ft 3-ins aft. She was found to be very wet, not rising easily to seas, and the fore turrets were washed down practically the whole time in a head sea. The mean period of roll was 14 seconds, and including raising steam, 876 tons of oil were burnt for 1,126 miles at 18 − 12 knots in winds of force 5 to 7. At Gibraltar the blades of a starboard turbine stripped, but the *Queen Elizabeth* could do 18 knots on her port engines thanks to her large rudders, and it was thus not of great importance to her employment at the Dardanelles.

The *Queen Elizabeth* was first in action on 25 February 1915 when she took part in the second bombardment of the entrance forts, the only successful day in the whole naval attack. She was anchored about 12,000 yards from Ertogrul, one of the only two works with any effective guns (two 9.4-in) and 12,400 yards from Sedd el Bahr, a quite obsolete fort. Her first six shots were fired at Sedd el Bahr, the next 18 in 77 minutes at Ertogrul and the last 7 at Sedd el Bahr. The sixteenth shot at Ertogrul apparently damaged the west gun, the seventeenth hit and dismounted the east gun and the last dismounted the west gun. This was very fine shooting as the theoretical chance of hitting one of the guns or mountings was at best only about 1 in 20. Common shell was fired with ¾ charges and to obtain the greatest possible accuracy the same gun was used throughout on each target, ramming distances were measured and the charges were from one lot of cordite. Individual laying was used to avoid inaccuracies between the Director sight and gun.

On March 5 the *Queen Elizabeth* opened the attack on the Narrows forts. These were far more formidable than those at the entrance and had a total of five 14-in and thirteen 9.4-in effective guns. The plan was that the *Queen Elizabeth* should fire over the Gallipoli peninsula at the forts on the European side of the Straits, using a cairn on top of a hill as an aiming mark, with spotting by aircraft and by three pre-dreadnoughts in the Straits. The advantages of this method were that the guns which could not reply offered a larger target than if attacked directly, and the *Queen Elizabeth* did not have to enter the Dardanelles where she might be exposed to mines and also be difficult to handle with only one set of engines. The success of such indirect fire depended entirely upon good spotting, and as usual in the naval attack on the Dardanelles, that from the seaplanes was useless, while the pre-dreadnoughts were spotting at 7 or 8 miles and entirely across the line of fire so that they could give no corrections for direction.

The *Queen Elizabeth* duly anchored and fired a total of 33 common shells in 4 hours 38 minutes at about 14,000 yards with ¾ charges and individual laying. Rumeli Medjidieh and Namazieh, with four and two effective 9.4-in respectively, were the targets ▷

H.M.S. Warspite in 1918, with the 6in. gun removed from the forecastle deck, and her topmast struck.

Two views of one of the 5th Battle Squadron seen from the Queen Elizabeth in 1917. Other ships are carrying out a 'throw-off' shoot, i.e. firing live ammunition but with sights 'thrown off' to avoid hitting the target.

The quarterdeck of the Queen Elizabeth in Scapa Flow in 1917, with the three Bellerophon Class Dreadnoughts in the background.

and 28 of the shells were fired at the former. No serious damage was done, though this was not then known. A field gun battery scored 17 or 18 unimportant hits on the *Queen Elizabeth*, before it was silenced by her secondary guns and by those of the *Inflexible* and *Prince George* that were in company with her.

It was decided to repeat this method of attack next day on Chemanlik, one of the forts on the Asiatic side which showed up well against the white houses of Chanak, and had one effective 14-in gun. The Turks meanwhile brought up the old battleship *Hairredin Barbarossa* and made preparations for her to fire over the peninsula from an anchorage above the Narrows. The result was one of the most bizarre encounters in ▷

H.M.S. Queen Elizabeth in 1918. Note the additional controls platforms on the mainmast. Aircraft platforms have not yet been added.

H. M. S. BARHAM in Battle Rig.

24   *H.M.S. Barham in 1918 with only one aircraft platform fitted.*

warship history, as this obsolete vessel, formerly the German *Kurfurst Friedrich Wilhelm* completed in 1894 and armed with six 11-in guns of that period elevating to 25°, was able, due to local geographical conditions, to endanger her formidable opponent.

The *Albion* was to spot inside the Straits with four other pre-dreadnoughts keeping down the fire from the intermediate defences, while the *Agamemnon* and *Ocean* covered the *Queen Elizabeth*. The latter duly anchored but three rounds thought to come from a howitzer battery were fired at her by the *Barbarossa*, and she moved 1,000 yards out. The *Barbarossa's* spotting position was discovered and fired on by the ships' secondary armament, so that it had to be abandoned. At 12.26 the *Queen Elizabeth* opened fire using ¾ charges at the limit of their range with Director laying and graphically extrapolated range tables as neither these nor the gun sights extended beyond 15° elevation. Jamming interfered with the *Albion's* signals and in 75 minutes only five common shell were fired, the last being thought to have hit a corner of Chemanlik at 18,400 yards.

Meanwhile a new spotting position had been found for the *Barbarossa* and the latter shifted her anchorage and reopened fire. She found the *Queen Elizabeth's* range in three rounds, and then fired some salvos and obtained three hits, but all on the armour below the water-line where no damage was

done. The *Barbarossa's* new spotting position was not discovered, and the *Queen Elizabeth* moved 3,100 yards out, well beyond the *Barbarossa's* range, though the latter fired two final shells at the *Agamemnon* before this ship also moved out. In all the *Barbarossa* expended twenty-one 11-in shells at about 16,500 yards, and it was doubtless fortunate for the *Queen Elizabeth* that none fell on her decks.

The *Queen Elizabeth* began again at Chemanlik at 3.32 with full charges and Director laying at 21,500 yards. Only two common shell, neither of which was spotted, were fired before bad light in the Straits put an end to proceedings. It was clearly a waste of time and ammunition to continue with indirect firing unless good aircraft spotting was available.

On 8 March the *Queen Elizabeth* engaged Rameli Medjidieh from inside the Straits, accompanied by four pre-dreadnoughts. There were rain squalls, the light was bad and spotting impossible, so that after firing eleven common shell with ¾ charges in about two-and-a-half hours at ranges of 12,400–16,900 yards, the *Queen Elizabeth* withdrew. On this occasion Vice-Admiral Carden, in command at the Dardanelles, flew his flag in her, and ten days later when the final naval attack was made, the *Queen Elizabeth* was the flagship of (acting) Vice Admiral de Robeck who had relieved Carden for reasons of ill-health.

In this attack on 18 March the *Queen*

Elizabeth, Inflexible and fourteen pre-dreadnoughts, of which four were French, took part inside the Straits. A field of 26 mines laid early on 8 March by the small Turkish steamer *Nusret* in waters thought to be clear, sank three pre-dreadnoughts and seriously damaged the *Inflexible*, while two more pre-dreadnoughts were put out of action by shells from the Narrows forts. These two and one of those sunk were French. The attack on the defences lasted nearly seven hours, and the *Queen Elizabeth* expended 178 15-in common shell and 101 6-in HE. The range for the 15-in probably varied from 14,000 to 17,000 yards, and most shells were fired at Anatoli Hamidieh, which mounted two 14-in and seven 9.4-in and was both the most powerful of the forts and the hardest to make out. A great deal of damage was done to the structure of the fort and one 15-in crater measured 39-ft x 32-ft x 9-ft deep, but only one 9.4-in was put out of action, and it is not certain that the *Queen Elizabeth* was responsible. Otherwise she engaged Chemanlik causing two magazine fires or explosions and putting one obsolete gun out of action, and also fired at Rumeli Medjidieh. The *Queen Elizabeth* was only hit by five 5.9-in howitzer shells which caused little damage and no casualties. Full charges were fired throughout with individual laying as the Director system was temporarily out of action, and the range was on the limit for ¾ charges at 15° elevation which was the ▷

H.M.S. Malaya in 1920, showing wartime additions including aircraft platforms on 'B' and 'Y' turrets.

maximum of the gun sights. The ship steamed slowly upstream and drifted down with the current. 'B' turret fired directly over 'A' for nearly the whole action, and 'A' gun-layer and the officer of the turret who relieved him at intervals, were exposed to the full blast of 'B' for most of the time, as the blast breeches of both guns in 'A' and the roller-blind blast screen of one, carried away.

The purely naval attack was now discontinued as little impression had been made on the Narrows forts and virtually none on the main minefield or on the intermediate batteries.

Between 25 April 1915 when the landings were made and 14 May when the *Queen Elizabeth* left for Scapa as the arrival of German submarines at the Dardanelles was expected, the ship was employed in support of the Army. On 25 April her 6-in guns were mainly used, firing 370 HE, while the 15-in expended only nine common and eight shrapnel shell, and from 26 to 28 April she fired 121 15-in (24 armour-piercing, 46 common, 51 shrapnel) and 406 6-in (163 HE, 243 shrapnel). The 15-in firing was by Director and nearly always with ¾ charges. Half charges were tried for a few rounds and found to give very accurate results up to their maximum of 12,000 yards. When off the Peninsula one turret always had shrapnel in the gun loading cage, and on 28 April one such shell burst and scattered its 13,770 balls in the right position to stop an attack

by a company of Turks. In the absence of a Director for the secondary armament it was very difficult to get the 6-in guns on to the correct target, and it was found necessary to show the target to a gunnery officer on the bridge, and then for him to fire the first marker shot personally

Kite-balloon spotting was now available, and it was possible to fire over the Peninsula with far better results than in March. On 26 April the *Hairredin Barbarossa* and her sister ship the *Torgut Reis* were driven off, and next day the third of three armour piercing shells fired at 18,000 yards, hit and sank the empty transport *Scutari of Nagara,* and five others still laden, were driven away upstream by three salvos. From 19 April the *Queen Elizabeth* was less active and her returns until 14 May show an expenditure of 86 15-in (three armour piercing, 72 common, 11 shrapnel) and 71 6-in (69 HE, two shrapnel). In four days she fired over the Peninsula at ships and also fired a few shells at her old target Rameli Medjidieh on two occasions, but had no success.

Lack of 15-in HE shells, of good ship to shore communications and often of good spotting, were serious handicaps. Also if Second World War experience is any guide, nothing like enough 15-in shells were fired. On one day, 19 February 1945, the American battleships *North Carolina* and *Washington* (each nine 16-in guns) fired 1,950 16-in shells between them, in support of the

landings on the small island of Iwo Jima which only measures 4½ x 2½ miles. This kind of expenditure was impossible in 1915 as there were not sufficient 15-in shells of any type, and the Admiralty had also ordered that the *Queen Elizabeth's* guns must not become worn.

JUTLAND

To do justice to the four ships of the 5th Battle Squadron that were present at Jutland — *Barham* (Rear-Admiral Evan-Thomas) *Valiant, Warspite* and *Malaya* — would require a complete account of the daylight fighting on 31 May 1916. The Squadron did not take part as intended as a fast wing of the battle fleet, but as a supporting force to the battlecruisers because the 3rd Battle Cruiser Squadron had gone to Scapa for exercises, and the 5th BS temporarily replaced them at Rosyth. Due to a signal made by flags at too great a distance to be seen, and not repeated by searchlight, the 5th BS were late in joining the action between the battlecruisers which began at 3.48, and it was not until ten minutes later that fire was opened on the light cruisers astern of the German line. At 4.08 the *Barham* began to engage the *Von der Tann*, and from then until 4.54 the 5th BS continued firing at the German battlecruisers whenever visibility was good enough. Initially the two rear ships, *Moltke* and *Von der Tann*, were engaged and later the others ▷

as well. This part of the battle was fought on a generally southward course, which led to the German battle fleet, and the British battlecruisers turned northward at 4.40 on sighting the latter, while the 5th BS did not do so until fourteen minutes later.

In the next phase of the action, which lasted until the British battle fleet deployed to port ahead of the German line at 6.15, the 5th BS engaged the German battlecruisers and their most powerful battleships of the 3rd Squadron. As previously, visibility was not always good enough for firing at ranges which were at times in excess of 20,000 yards, while for 31 minutes the British battlecruisers withdrew from the action to gain a favourable position ahead. On the British forces joining, the battlecruisers were able to take station ahead of the battle fleet, but the 5th BS could not do so and turned to join at the rear of the line. While turning the *Warspite's* helm jammed and she circled round under a very heavy fire from some of the German battleships, but was able to get away though she did not rejoin the squadron. Of the other three ships, the *Barham* and *Valiant* fired effectively but briefly at German battleships at about 7.15.

Such are the barest outlines of the 5th Battle Squadron's activities in the Battle of Jutland. A detailed study of this action based on a thorough re-examination of British and German reports, shows that of the 104 hits by heavy shells on German battleships and battlecruisers, 31 came from the 5th BS. Visibility conditions when firing were on average worse for them than for any other British squadron, and the average range also greater. The total 15-in ammunition expenditure by the 5th BS was 1,099 made up as follows:
Barham, 337 (136 APC, 201 CPC); *Valiant*, 278 APC, 10 CPC); *Warspite*, 259; *Malaya*, 215.

The German reports from those of the light cruiser *Pillau*, one of the 5th Battle Squadron's first targets, to those of the battleship *Helgoland*, which was one of the last, are unanimous in praising the shooting of this squadron, the salvos having an extremely small spread at all ranges, and it may be that more hits would have been made if the spread had been larger. Although the poor quality of the British armour piercing shells much reduced the value of the hits on armour, and in the whole battle only two of these shells, one from the *Revenge* and one from the *Barham* or *Valiant*, actually pierced armour of 6-in and over and burst inside, the 15-in shells did great damage to the unarmoured parts of the German ships. Perhaps the most destructive was one on the *Seydlitz* at 5.06 from either the *Barham* or *Valiant*. This pierced the forecastle deck about 6-ft on the port side of the centre line and 65—70-ft from the bows, bursting above the upper deck and 6-ft from the starboard side. A hole of about 10-ft x 13-ft was torn in the skin

plating between the battery and forecastle decks and large quantities of water poured in at high speed. Aided by the damage from four other hits by the 5th BS in this part of the ship, water gradually spread to all forward compartments above the armour deck. This increased the *Seydlitz's* draught forward, and by 9 pm on 31 May the hole in the side caused by this shell was very near the then water-line, and as the *Seydlitz* continued to sink deeper forward water was able to enter the ship further aft, and to find its way below the armour deck via leaking cable glands, voice pipes, ventilation trunks and hatches. Although the *Seydlitz* had previously been torpedoed, it was the effect of the hit at 5.06 that was chiefly responsible for her nearly sinking.

The heaviest German guns at Jutland were 12-in and it was probably fortunate for the 5th BS that the *Bayern* with her 15-in guns, had not completed her working up period. The *Valiant* was never hit, but the *Warspite* received at least thirteen heavy and five 5.9-in hits after her helm jammed. Apart from this the *Warspite* was hit twice by heavy shells, the *Barham* six times and the *Malaya* seven. Of the total of 28 heavy hits, six were on the side armour. The worst of these pierced the upper part of the *Warspite's* belt after her helm jammed, wrecking the port feed tank and did much damage, so that considerable quantities of water entered the port wing engine room. The mean armour thickness was 7½-ins where ▷

H.M.S. Queen Elizabeth 1919.

The mainmast and tripod of the Queen Elizabeth in 1917.

H.M.S. Barham as she appeared in 1917, with added searchlight and control positions on the mainmast.

H.M.S. QUEEN ELIZABETH IN 1918.

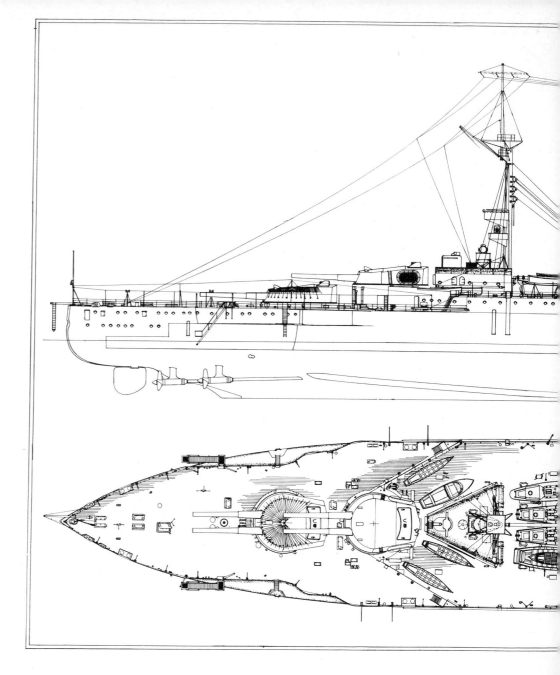

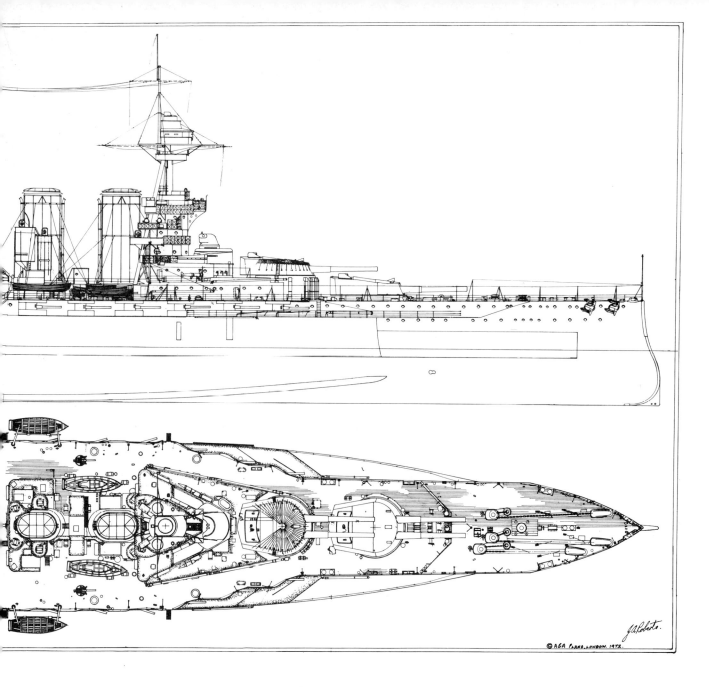

©AGA PLANS, LONDON. 1972.

33

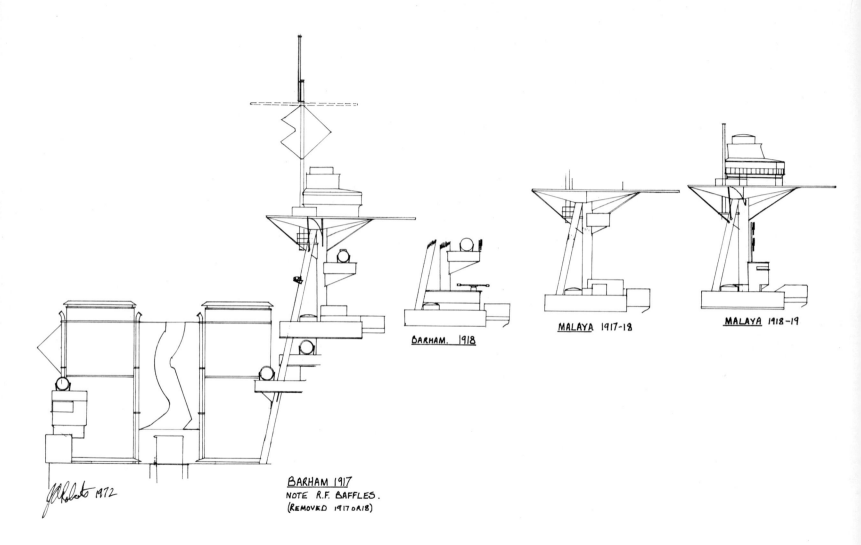

BARHAM. 1918

MALAYA 1917-18

MALAYA 1918-19

BARHAM 1917
NOTE R.F. BAFFLES.
(REMOVED 1917 OR18)

34

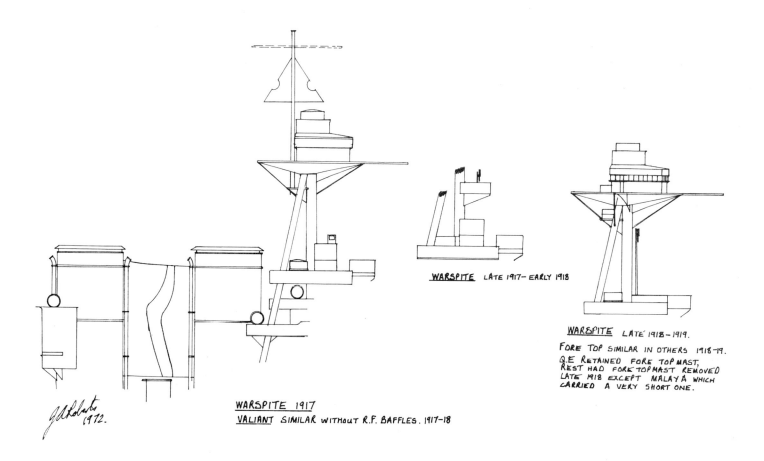

J.A.Roberts
1972.

WARSPITE LATE 1917 — EARLY 1918

WARSPITE 1917
VALIANT SIMILAR WITHOUT R.F. BAFFLES. 1917-18

WARSPITE LATE 1918 — 1919.

FORE TOP SIMILAR IN OTHERS 1918-19.
Q.E RETAINED FORE TOP MAST,
REST HAD FORE TOP MAST REMOVED
LATE 1918 EXCEPT MALAYA WHICH
CARRIED A VERY SHORT ONE.

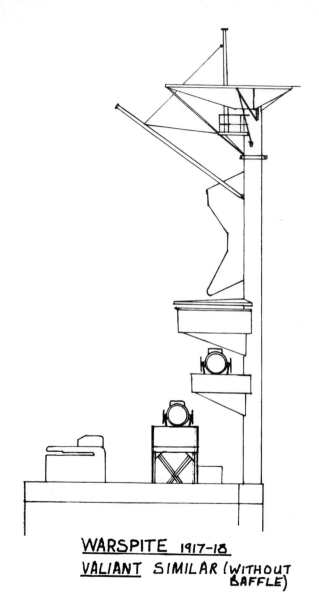

WARSPITE 1917-18
VALIANT SIMILAR (WITHOUT BAFFLE)

36

BARHAM 1917-18

NOTE CANVAS RANGE FINDER BAFFLES
(REMOVED 1917 OR 18)

MALAYA SIMILAR (WITHOUT BAFFLES)

GAFFS AS IN 1916.

Q.E. AFTER SUPERSTRUCTURE A MAIN DRAWING DURIN 1917-18 PERIOD.

Q.E WAS ONLY MEMBER OF CLASS TO RETAIN MAIN TOPMAST DURING 1917-1919.

JRoberts
1972.

A PART OF H.M.S. "QUEEN ELIZABETH."

H.M.S. Queen Elizabeth as she appeared in 1919 with all her wartime modifications.

hit, and this shell illustrates why the 13-in belt armour should have been taken to the main deck. Two other shells pierced the *Warspite's* 6-in upper side armour at this time, and caused a good deal of damage. One of the earlier hits on the *Warspite* pierced the 6-in side armour aft with local damage, and the other hits on side armour were on the *Malaya's* 6-in upper belt and on the *Barham's* main belt below water, in neither case with much effect.

In the *Malaya*. 'X' turret roof was hit and a very small hole made, but the turret continued in action. There were three hits well below water in this ship, and one of these which distorted the torpedo bulkhead, caused much flooding so that the *Malaya* listed about 4⁰, and eventually oil fuel ▷

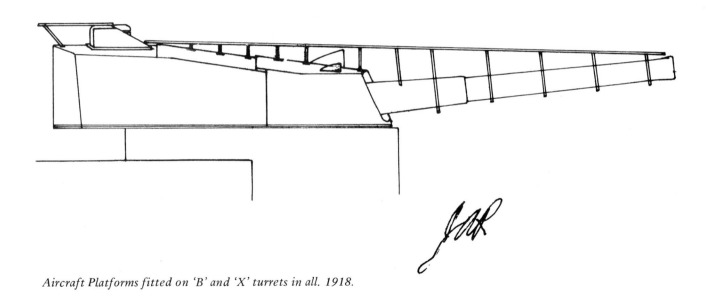

Aircraft Platforms fitted on 'B' and 'X' turrets in all. 1918.

found its way into the forward boiler room which had to be shut down during the return to harbour.

Of the other 18 hits, two were very dangerous. A shell pierced the 1-in forecastle deck near No. 3 starboard 6-in gun in the *Malaya* and burst 7-ft from impact. It was the practice to have twelve ready charges per 6-in gun stowed in rectangular 'W' cases, which held four charges each and were not fireproof. Shell fragments ignited the charges in some of these cases, and the resultant cordite fire spread along the whole starboard battery. The flash passed down the forward 6-in hoist into the 6-in shell room, and was only prevented from igniting ten 6-in cartridges ready for hoisting by the prompt action of P.O. Day and L/S Watson in removing smouldering debris. If these cartridges had ignited, the 6-in magazine above the shell room and with two handing scuttles open to the latter, would have exploded, followed by the adjacent forward 15-in magazines and the *Malaya* would have been lost.

In the *Barham* a shell pierced the 1¼-in upper deck where it formed the glacis to No. 2 starboard 6-in gun, and burst 15-ft from impact at the main deck. Very great damage was done, and the flash of the burst passed via the 6-in hand-ups to the battery, where it ignited some charges by No. 2 starboard gun, and also passed down a trunk to the dynamo room on the platform deck. The explosion blew a hole 7-ft x

7-ft in the 3/8-in main deck and part of the shell head went through the 1-in middle deck into the lower conning tower. A fragment also went through the middle deck and 3/8-in lower deck into the 6-in magazine, and other fragments that holed the middle deck put one of the hydraulic pumps out of action, but the remaining three pumps kept all four turrets going.

Apart from these two very dangerous hits, a shell that burst on the *Warspite's* forecastle deck sent flash through a small hole into the 6-in battery and ignited the charges in five 'W' cases, and the base plug of another shell on this ship that struck the upper deck between the after barbettes, went through the middle deck into 'X' magazine cooler.

Only one of the 5.9-in hits on the *Warspite* was important, and this bulged the barrel of the left gun in 'Y' turret and put the gun out of action.

The jamming of the *Warspite's* helm was due to the continued use of the steering engine under heavy loads from the high speed maintained, overheating the thrust shaft. This slowed the engine down and prevented the differential valve gear responding to the movement of the steering wheel and the latter was thus hard to move. Very great force was used on the wheels in the upper and lower conning tower, with the result that control of the steering from these positions was rendered useless. A very moderate extemporised water supply cooled the thrust

shaft, and the steering engine then worked satisfactorily, but the *Warspite* had now to be steered from the position in the engine room. Somewhat similar trouble had in fact occurred in the *Valiant* on 4 May 1916.

The German 3rd Squadron were able to keep the 5th BS in range for a considerable time between 4.54 and 6.15 and this was difficult to explain if the *Queen Elizabeths* were believed to be 25 knot ships. In fact the 5th Battle Squadron's speed in this period of the action was about 23.8 knots while the two leading German battleships, the *Konig* and *Grosser Kurfurst*, did not appreciably exceed 22 knots and the third ship, the *Markgraf*, did not attain this speed. The Germans were steering a somewhat converging course which allowed them to keep in range at the price of all but the forward turrets eventually being unable to bear.

APPEARANCE CHANGES 1914-1918

Queen Elizabeth was the only one of the class to mount her four additional 6-in guns in the main deck battery aft, and these were removed in 1915 and replaced by single 6-in guns in shields on the forecastle deck. Others of the class were completed with this arrangement, but in 1917—18 the growing danger of air attack led to these guns being replaced by 3-in anti-aircraft guns.

Queen Elizabeth differed from all the others in having a sternwalk, but this was ▷

removed in 1915 or early 1916. In common with the others she had her searchlights put into towers on the second funnel in 1916-17. *Barham* initially had a searchlight platform on the forebridge but this distinctive feature was replaced by a rangefinder in 1917. *Warspite* was fitted with range-finding baffles to confuse German range-takers in 1917-18; these were enormous flanges between the funnels and on the mainmast, but they proved useless as the Germans used stereo-scopic rangefinders.

In 1917-18 all ships of the class received a searchlight platform and additional control platform on the mainmast. At this time also the turrets were marked with deflection scales and range-clocks were fitted on masts; both devices were aids to fire-control in that they passed on target-information rapidly to squadron-mates even if other forms of signalling had broken down. By mid-1918 all of the class were being fitted with aircraft platforms on 'B' and 'X' turrets, allowing them to fly off a recon-naissance aircraft and a fighter.

CONCLUSION

In 1920 plans were drawn up for re-armouring the *Queen Elizabeths,* but these were shelved after the Washington Treaty. In 1926—28 all five were taken in hand for modernisation, which involved extensions to the bridgework and the addition of anti-torpedo "bulges". The bulges also had the valuable effect of ▷

Queen Elizabeth in November 1927 after her funnels had been trunked to reduce smoke interference. Note that she has also been fitted with anti-torpedo bulges.

reducing the maximum draught and off-setting the great increase over designed displacement mentioned earlier. To reduce smoke interference the forward funnel in each ship was trunked into the second, in a manner reminiscent of Japanese ships.

Between 1933 and 1938 the *Warspite, Valiant* and *Queen Elizabeth* were taken in hand for rebuilding on a scale which left very little of the old ships, apart from the 15-in turrets, while *Malaya* and *Barham* had a limited modernisation to render them fit for front-line duties. Once again the class set up a magnificent record, although *Barham* blew up with heavy loss of life after being torpedoed in 1941.

Although the *Queen Elizabeths* performed so well in the 1914-1918 War it must always be regretted that they were not designed to a 5,000 or 6,000-ton greater displacement which could have produced near perfection for the time, even though the necessary additional beam would have meant some more large floating docks. □

Warspite in July 1937, showing how she had been completely altered. Queen Elizabeth and Valiant were similarly altered in 1938–41.

Careers:

Barham

19 Aug. 1915 Commissioned at Clydebank by Captain Craig.

28 Aug. Docked at Liverpool.

1 Oct. 1915 Departed from Liverpool and hoisted Flag of Rear-Admiral Evan-Thomas (5th Battle Squadron).

2 Oct. Arrived at Scapa Flow and began her gunnery trials.

3 Dec. Collided with *Warspite,* and was holed on her starboard side abreast of the quarterdeck.

8 Dec. to 23 Dec. Under repair at Cromarty and Invergordon.

31 May 1916 Battle of Jutland.

3 June 1916 Admiral and his staff left the ship for duration of her repairs.

5 June Docked at Devonport.

5 July Left Devonport and ran her full speed trials in Bute Sound the next day.

25 Feb. 1917 Docked at Cromarty for refit.

12 March Left Invergordon at end of her refit.

8 Oct. Struck the Flag of Vice-Admiral Sir Hugh Evan-Thomas.

23 Oct. Rehoisted the Flag.

7 Feb. 1918 Struck the Flag, and arrived at Rosyth for refit the following day.

23 Feb. Left Rosyth to return to 5th Battle Squadron and rehoisted Vice-Admiral Sir Hugh Evan-Thomas' Flag.

17 March Captain Craig relieved by Captain Buller.

1 Oct. Vice-Adm. Sir Hugh Evan-Thomas relieved by V-Adm. A.C. Leveson.

11 Nov. Cessation of hostilities.

1920-1924 Flagship of 1st Battle Squadron of Atlantic Fleet.

1924-27 Mediterranean Fleet.

1927 1928 Refitted, and emerged with anti-torpedo 'bulges', funnels trunked together etc.

1928-29 Mediterranean Fleet.

1929-1930 Atlantic Fleet.

1930-1933 Refitted and re-engined.

1933-1935 Home Fleet

1935-1939 Mediterranean Fleet, but rejoined Home Fleet on outbreak of war.

28 Dec. 1939 Torpedoed by U.30 north of Hebrides.

Dec. 39—Mar. 40 Under repair at Liverpool.

28 Mar. 1941 Battle of Cape Matapan.

27 May. Damaged by aircraft attack off Crete.

July Rejoined Mediterranean Fleet after repairs at Durban.

25 Nov. 1941 Torpedoed and sunk by U-boat, with heavy loss of life following a large explosion.

Malaya

1 Feb. 1916 Commissioned at Newcastle-upon-Tyne.

17 Feb. Left for Scapa, and arrived the following day to join 5th Battle Squadron.

4 July Completed repairs to damage.

22 Nov. 1918 In collision with destroyer *Penn* and sustained slight damage on port quarter.

April 1919 Visit to Cherbourg for Peace Celebrations.

1920 Conveyed Allied Disarmament Commission on its inspection of German ports.

1921 Carried Prince Arthur of Connaught to India and paid courtesy visit to Malaya.

1920-1924 Atlantic Fleet.

1922 Carried former Sultan of Turkey to exile.

1924-1927 Mediterranean Fleet, 1st Battle Squadron.

1927-1929 Refitted (as *Barham*).

1920-1930 Mediterranean Fleet.

1930-1932 Atlantic Fleet.

1932-1934 Home Fleet.

1934-1936 Refitted with aircraft hangars and increased anti-aircraft armament.

1937-1939 Mediterranean Fleet.

Sept. 1939-Mar. 1940 Convoy and patrol duties in North Atlantic.

Mar. 1940 Transferred to Mediterranean.

9 July 1940 Action with Italian Fleet off Calabria.

1941 Flagship of Force 'H'.

June 1944 Bombarding ship at Normandy.

1945 Paid off into Reserve.

12 Apr. 1948 Arrived at Faslane for scrapping.

Queen Elizabeth

22 Dec. 1914 Commissioned by Captain ▷

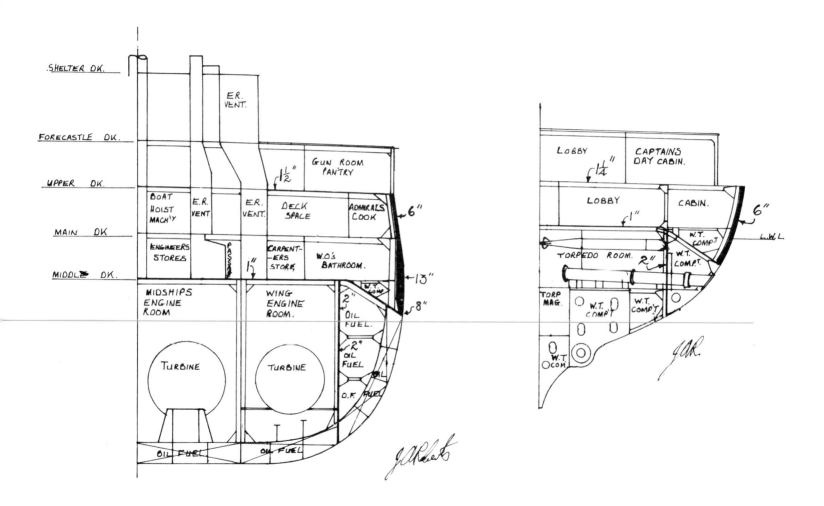

SHELTER DK.

E.R. VENT.

FORECASTLE DK.

UPPER DK.

MAIN DK.

MIDDLE DK.

GUN ROOM PAN'TRY

BOAT HOIST MACH'Y

E.R. VENT.

E.R. VENT.

$1\frac{1}{2}''$

DECK SPACE

ADMIRALS CAB'N

6"

ENGINEERS STORES

PASSAGE

CARPENT-ERS STORE

W.O's BATHROOM.

1"

W.T. COMP'T

13"

MIDSHIPS ENGINE ROOM

WING ENGINE ROOM.

2" OIL FUEL

8"

TURBINE

TURBINE

2" OIL FUEL

OIL

O.F. FUEL

OIL FUEL

OIL FUEL

LOBBY

CAPTAINS DAY CABIN.

$1\frac{1}{4}''$

LOBBY

CABIN.

1"

6"

W.T. COMP'T

L.W.L

TORPEDO ROOM.

2"

W.T. COMP'T

TORP MAG.

W.T. COMP'T

W.T. COMP'T

W.T. COM'

43

▷ Hope at Portsmouth.
5 Feb. 1915 Arrived at Gibraltar.
18 Feb. Left Gibraltar.
20 Feb Arrived at Tenedos.
14 May 1915 Struck Admiral de Robeck's Flag at Mudros and left for Gibraltar the same day.
1915 Arrived at Gibraltar and left the following day.
26 May Arrived at Scapa Flow and joined 5th Battle Squadron.
22 May 1916 Arrived at Rosyth for refit.
4 June 1916 Hoisted Flag of Rear-Admiral Evan-Thomas while *Barham* was under repair.
25 June Struck Admiral's Flag.
3 July Rehoisted Flag.
11 July Struck Flag of V-Adm. Sir Hugh Evan-Thomas for last time and underwent a refit as Fleet Flagship.
Feb. 1917 Became Fleet Flagship.
21-24 June Visited by HM King George V during his visit to the Grand Fleet.
9-10 Sept. Temporarily wore the Flag of Admiral Mayo, USN.
15 Nov. 1918 German flag-officers arrived on board to negotiate the surrender of the High Seas Fleet.
July 1919-1924 Flagship of Atlantic Fleet.
July 1924-1926 Flagship of Mediterranean Fleet.
1926-1927 Refitted as *Barham*.
1927-1929 Mediterranean Fleet.
1929 Atlantic Fleet.
1929-1937 Mediterranean Fleet.
Aug. 1937-Jan 1941 Under reconstruction

at Portsmouth.
Jan 1941 Home Fleet at Scapa.
May 1941 Joined Mediterranean Fleet (1st Battle Squadron).
19 Dec. 1941 Severely damaged by Italian limpet mines in Alexandria.
Dec. 1941-June 1943 Under repair, first at Alexandria, then in U.S.A.
Jan 1944-July 1945 1st Battle Squadron, Eastern Fleet.
Aug. 1945 Joined Reserve Fleet at Rosyth.
7 July 1948 Arrived at Dalmuir for scrapping.

Valiant

.**13 Jan. 1916** Commissioned at Govan by Captain Woolcombe.
1 Feb. Left Govan to carry out final trials.
5 Feb. Carried out speed and gunnery trials at Greenock.
3 Mar. Arrived at Scapa Flow to join 5th Battle Squadron.
31 May Battle of Jutland.
24 Aug. Collided with *Warspite*, striking her abreast of the foremast funnel, and sustaining damage to her own stern (foremost watertight compartment flooded).
26 Aug.-18 Sept. Under repair at Cromarty.
11 Nov. 1918 Cessation of hostilities.
21 Dec. Visited by Admiral of the Fleet Lord Fisher of Kilverstone.
1919-1924 1st Battle Squadron, Atlantic Fleet.
1924-1929 Mediterranean Fleet.

1929-1930 Refitted as *Barham*.
1930-1932 Atlantic Fleet.
1932-1935 Home Fleet
1935-1937 Mediterranean Fleet
1937-1939 Under reconstruction at Portsmouth in similar manner to *Queen Elizabeth*.
Dec. 1939 Began working up in West Indies.
Feb. 1940 Joined Home Fleet.
Aug. 1940 Transferred to Mediterranean Fleet.
16 Dec. 1940 Bombarded Valona.
28 Mar. 1941 Battle of Cape Matapan.
May 1941 Slightly damaged by air attack of Crete.
19 Dec. 1941 With *Queen Elizabeth* seriously damaged by Italian limpet mines in Alexandria.
Apr. 1942 Joined Eastern Fleet.
2 June 1943 Refitted.
6 Dec. 1943 Mediterranean, including Salerno Landings.
Jan. 1944 Joined Eastern Fleet.
1945 Seriously damaged in accidental flooding of a floating dock at Trincomalee.
July 1945 Paid off for refit, and joined Imperieuse training establishment at Devonport.
12 Nov. 1948 Arrived at Cairnryan for scrapping (hull towed to Troon for further demolition in 1950).

Warspite
8 Mar. 1915 Commissioned at Devonport by Captain Philpotts.
5 Apr. Embarked crew. ▷

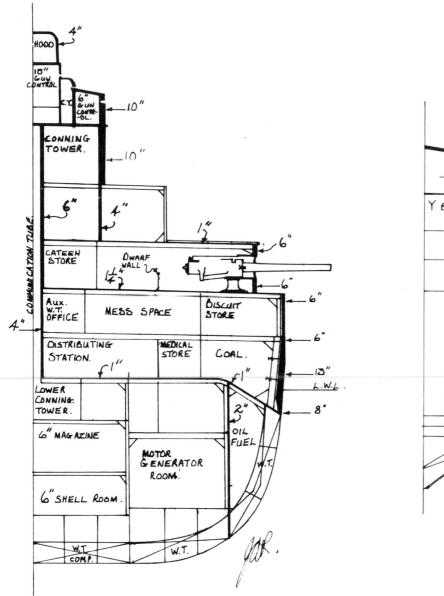

4" HOOD

15" GUN CONTROL

C.T.

6" GUN CONTROL

10"

CONNING TOWER.

10"

6"

4"

COMMUNICATION TUBE.

CATEEN STORE

DWARF WALL

1"

1¼"

6"

6"

AUX. W.T. OFFICE

MESS SPACE

BISCUIT STORE

6"

DISTRIBUTING STATION.

MEDICAL STORE

COAL.

6"

1"

1"

13"

L.W.L.

LOWER CONNING TOWER.

8"

2"

OIL FUEL

W.T.

6" MAGAZINE

MOTOR GENERATOR ROOM.

6" SHELL ROOM.

W.T. COMP.

W.T.

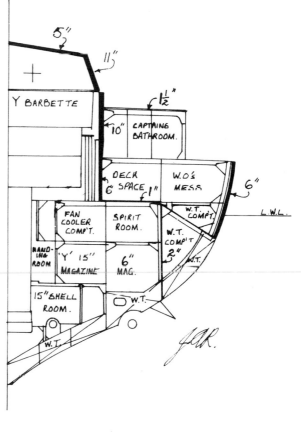

5"

11"

Y BARBETTE

1½"

10"

CAPTAINS BATHROOM.

DECK SPACE

6"

1"

W.O's MESS

6"

FAN COOLER COMP'T.

SPIRIT ROOM.

W.T. COMPT.

L.W.L.

BAND-ING ROOM

'Y' 15" MAGAZINE

6" MAG.

W.T. COMPT.

2"

W.T.

15" SHELL ROOM.

W.T.

W.T.

45

▷ **8 Apr.** Carried out gunnery and steaming trials.
13 Apr. Arrived at Scapa Flow and joined 5th Battle Squadron.
16 Sept. Grounded.
17-22 Sept. Under repair at Rosyth.
22 Sept.—20 Nov. Under repair at Jarrow.
3 Dec. In collision with *Barham.*
11-21 Dec. Refitting at Devonport.
31 May 1916 Battle of Jutland.
1 June Arrived at 1.30 at Rosyth for docking.
23 July Arrived at Scapa Flow following repairs.
24 Aug. In collision with *Valiant*, with serious damages.
26 Aug—28 Sept. Under repair at Rosyth.
19 Dec. Captain Philpotts relieved by Captain de Barolome.
11 June 1917 In minor collision with a destroyer.

8 Mar. 1937 Began trials.
7 Feb. 1918 Hoisted Flag of Vice-Admiral commanding 5th Battle Squadron.
12 Mar.—6 May Refitted at Rosyth.
3 June Captain de Barolome relieved by Captain Lynes.
11 Nov. Cessation of hostilities.
1919-1924 1st Battle Squadron, Atlantic Fleet.
1924-1926 Refitted as *Barham.*
1926-1930 Mediterranean Fleet
1930-1932 Atlantic Fleet.
1932-1934 Home Fleet (paid off 15 Dec. 1933).
1934-1937 Under reconstruction at Portsmouth.
1937-1939 Flagship of Mediterranean Fleet.
13 Apr. 1940 Second Battle of Narvik.
11 May 1940 Hoisted Flag of Admiral Cunningham as C-in-c, Mediterranean Fleet.

28 Mar. 1941 Battle of Cape Matapan.
22 May 1941 Damaged by aircraft attack off Crete.
8 Dec. 1941 Under repair at Seattle, U.S.A.
1942-1943 Eastern Fleet, then to Mediterranean for Salerno landings.
19 Sept. 1943 Severely damaged by German glider-bombs.
Sept 1943-Apr. 1944 Under repair at Rosyth.
6 June 1944 D-Day bombardment.
13 June Damaged by magnetic mine off Harwich.
25 Aug. Bombarded Brest.
1 Nov. Supported Walcheren landing.
1 Feb. 1945 Paid off into Reserve Category C.
31 July 1946 Approval given for scrapping.
12 Mar. 1947 Left Portsmouth in tow for Faslane.
23 Apr. After breaking her tow ran aground in Prussia Cove.
1956 Last portions of the *Warspite* removed. □

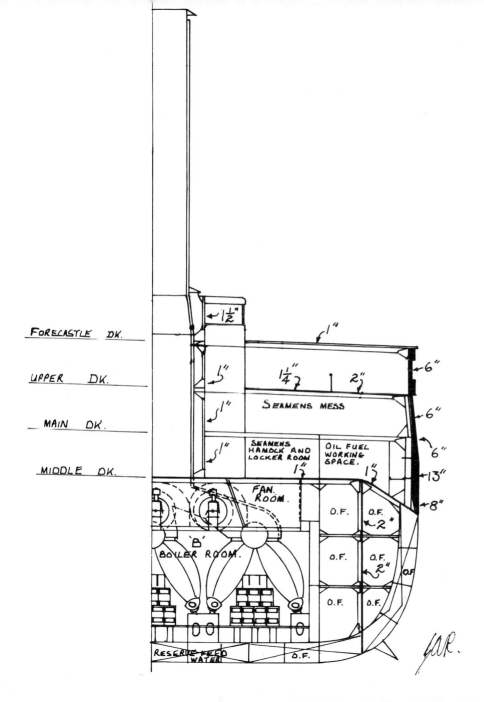

FORECASTLE DK.

UPPER DK.

MAIN DK.

MIDDLE DK.

1½"

1"

1"

1"

1"

1¼"

2"

6"

6"

6"

13"

8"

SEAMENS MESS

SEAMENS HAMOCK AND LOCKER ROOM

OIL FUEL WORKING SPACE.

1"

1"

FAN. ROOM.

'B' BOILER ROOM.

O.F.

O.F.

2"

O.F.

O.F.

2"

O.F.

O.F.

O.F.

RESERVE FEED WATER

O.F.

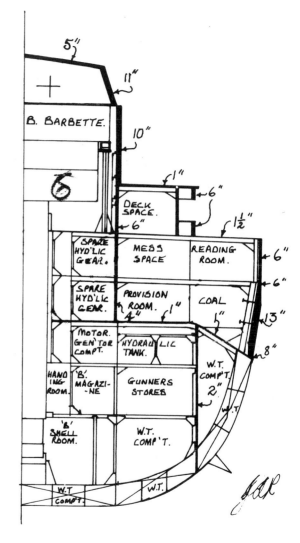

5"

11"

B. BARBETTE.

10"

1"

6"

1½"

DECK SPACE.

6"

SPARE HYD'LIC GEAR.

MESS SPACE

READING ROOM.

6"

6"

SPARE HYD'LIC GEAR.

PROVISION ROOM.

4"

1"

COAL

1"

13"

MOTOR. GEN'TOR COMPT.

HYDRAULIC TANK.

8"

HAND ING ROOM.

'B' MAGAZI-NE

GUNNERS STORES

W.T. COMP'T

2"

W.T.

'B' SHELL ROOM.

W.T. COMP'T.

W.T. COMP'T

W.T.

47

BARHAM

1. Forecastle deck
2. 'A' Turret
3. 'B' Turret.
4. Aircraft flying off Platforms.
5. Conning Tower.
6. Revolving 15ft Range Finder Hood.
7. Chart House and searchlight Platform.
8. Compass Platform.
9. 9ft Range Finder.
10. 36" searchlights (11 in number)
11. Spotting Top.
12. Main 15" Director.
13. 6" Directors (P & S).
14. Compass Platform.
15. Lower Searchlight platform.
16. Awning Room. (Beef screen under).
17. Searchlight Control Platforms.
18. Boats.
19. Main Derrick.
20. Starfish.

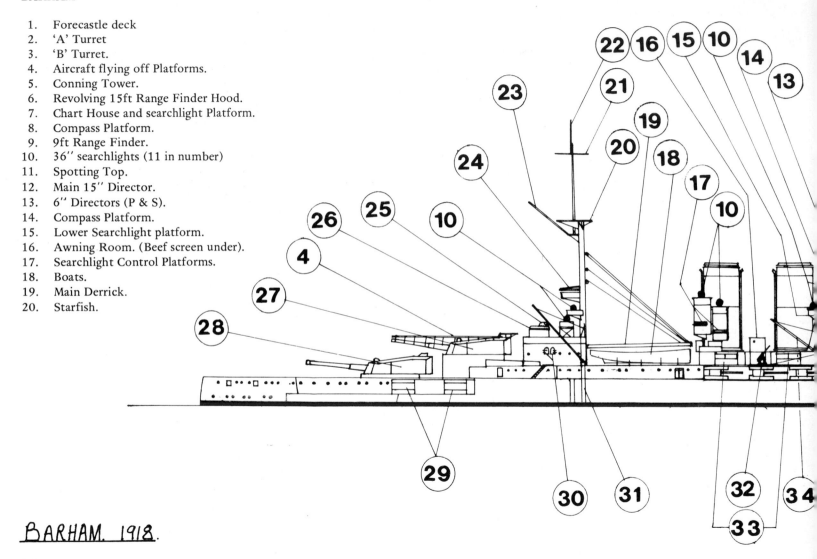

BARHAM. 1918.

48

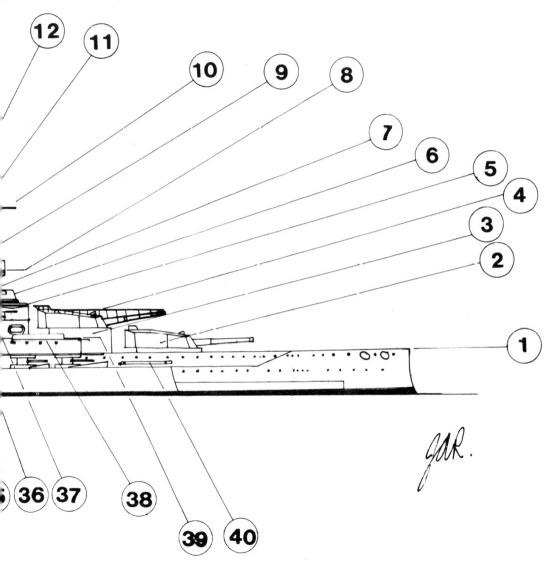

21. Yard.
22. Flagstaff.
23. Gaff.
24. Searchlight control Platform.
25. Revolving Range Finder Hood.
26. Torpedo Control Tower.
27. 'X' Turret.
28. 'Y' Turret.
29. Redundant 6" casemates.
30. Doors to E.R. Vents.
31. Refuse shoot.
32. 3" A/A gun (P & S)
33. B.R. Vents.
34. 34' derrick.
35. 6" Battery.
36. Conning Tower Platform.
37. Night gun control.
38. 40' derrick.
39. For'd Shelter deck.
40. Paravane Boom.

Bibliography

Details of Q.E's and armament etc.
Ships Covers for class
British Naval Construction 1914—1918
Technical History Series
Turbine Manual 1920
Hydraulic Manual 15" Mark I
Gunnery Manual 1915.
Ammunition Manual 1915
Final report Projectile Committee 1917
Torpedo School Reports 1913—1919.
Admiralty Dock Books

Details of German ships and designs
Schiffbau 1921
Trans. I.N.A. Description SMS *'Baden'*
German ships Damage reports and drawings.
1914—1918 British Intelligence material.
Specification (Bauvorschrift) for SMS *'Derfflinger'*.
'Deutsche Grosskampfschiffe' 1915—1918,
by Forstmeier and Breyer.
Manual for 38 cm. SKL/45 in Drk. L.C./ 1913.
'Die Entwicklung des Unterwasserschutzes in .der Deutschen Kriegsmarine'. Burkhardt in Marine Rundschau 1961.

U.S. and Japanese ships and guns.
From Lt. Com. R.O. Dulin, USN.

Dardanelles
The Mitchell Report.
P.R.O. ADM 137/38, 39, 109, 110, 254, 779, 2118.
ADM 116/1434
'Der Krieg zur See 1914—1918'. Mediterranean and Marmora volumes.
Marine Rundschau 1925 (Weniger).

Jutland
From my MS — Principal sources for 5th BS — German ships' war diaries, battle and damage reports.
'Jutland Despatches'.
Final Report Projectile Committee 1917.
Grand Fleet Gunnery & Torpedo Memoranda.
Jellicoe Papers in BM. Add. MSS.
P.R.O. CAB 45/269.
P.R.O. ADM 1./8460
ADM 137/301, 302, 2028. (This last contains 'Warspite' steering troubles).